P9-CRZ-576

YOU MUST REMEMBER THIS

1931

MILESTONES, MEMORIES,
TRIVIA AND FACTS, NEWS EVENTS,
PROMINENT PERSONALITIES &
SPORTS HIGHLIGHTS OF THE YEAR

TO :

FROM :

MESSAGE :

selected and researched
by
betsy dexter

WARNER TREASURES™

PUBLISHED BY WARNER BOOKS

A TIME WARNER COMPANY

Warner Books, Inc.
1271 Avenue of the Americas
New York, New York 10020

Warner Treasures is a
trademark of Warner Books, Inc.

A Time Warner Company

DESIGN:
CAROL BOKUNIEWICZ DESIGN
PRINTED IN SINGAPORE
FIRST PRINTING: SEPTEMBER 1996
10 9 8 7 6 5 4 3 2 1
ISBN: 0-446-91143-7

The Depression still dominated national
consciousness, as Congress and President Hoover struggled to turn the country around. Unemployment reached 5 million. Bank panic spread coast to coast.

President Hoover proposed a one-year moratorium on all World War I debts and reparations in order to break the worldwide depression. Congress and U.S. financial leaders supported the move.

Al "Scarface" Capone,

Chicago's all-powerful mob boss, found himself imprisoned for income tax evasion. His annual income, at the time of his arrest, was estimated at $20 million.

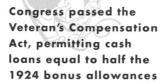

AL CAPONE

Congress passed the Veteran's Compensation Act, permitting cash loans equal to half the 1924 bonus allowances to each soldier.

The George Washington Memorial Bridge was completed. The 1,644-foot-long architectural wonder spanned the Hudson River, connecting New York and New Jersey for the first time.

newsreel

THE UNITED STATES CENSUS REPORTED THAT THE COUNTRY NOW HAD 19,700 MILLIONAIRES.

In the Mukden Incident, the Japanese army seized the massive Chinese arsenal at Mukden, going on to overrun southern Manchuria.

Clad in loincloth and shawl, **Mahatma Gandhi** paid a visit to King George V and Queen Mary in Buckingham Palace. Asked if the king had given any encouragement for Indian independence, Gandhi replied, "Only God gives encouragement, not kings." Shortly afterward, Gandhi was barred from meeting with the Pope—for refusing to wear Western clothes.

In London, police clashed with 5,000 unemployed protesters. The out-of-work Brits rioted to demonstrate their opposition to reduction in government benefits.

headlines

international

A devastating earthquake destroyed the entire city of Managua, Nicaragua. Rescuers found 1,100 dead among the rubble.

In Spain, Niceto Alcalá Zamora was elected the first constitutional President of Spain. Called the "father of the Spanish Republic," Alcalá Zamora led the successful revolutionary movement to victory under the Republican banner.

French divers found $5 million in gold bullion on remains of the sunken ocean liner *Egypt*.

JOSEPH STALIN

In Soviet Russia, Premier **Stalin** ruled with an iron hand. Charging that meat and vegetable trusts were clogged with "anti-Soviet agents," Stalin ordered 48 offenders shot on sight. In order to eat, Russian workers had to prove they were employed at a factory or business sanctioned by the government. An estimated 663,200 Russian Soviets now languished in penal camps.

THE MEDIAN AGE FOR AMERICAN NEWLYWEDS WAS 24.3 FOR THE GROOM, 21.3 FOR THE BLUSHING BRIDE.

Congress voted on March 3 to make Francis Scott Key's **"Star Spangled Banner"** the national anthem. The anthem took its melody from an old English drinking song.

On December 31, Pope Pius XI issued an encyclical denouncing extramarital sex, all forms of birth control, and divorce.

In New York City, Wiley Post and Harold Gatto were given a ticker tape parade after completing a round-the-world flight in record time. The pair took off from Roosevelt Field in their plane, the *Winnie Mae*, and landed in the same field 8 days, 15 hours, and 51 minutes later.

The appearance of **Dick Tracy** by cartoonist Chester Gould introduced three new elements—gadgetry, humor, and science fiction—that became a mainstay of comic strips.

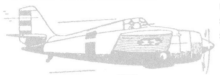

Hattie T. Caraway of Arkansas became the first woman elected to the U.S. Senate.

The Nobel Peace Prize was awarded to two Americans, Jane Addams and Dr. Nicholas Murray Butler. The 71-year-old Miss Addams led the Women's League for Peace and Freedom. Butler, president of Columbia University, helped found the Carnegie Endowment for International Peace. Both recipients gave away their prize money.

'31 cultural milestones

TWA began the first air-freight service with a shipment of cows from St. Louis to Newark.

BUCK ROGERS

8

ED SULLIVAN

radio

TOP NEW SHOWS

"The Ed Sullivan Show"

"The March of Time" with Ted Husing

"The Eddie Cantor Show"

"Singing Lady" with Irene Wicker

"Buck Rogers"

"Skippy," with Franklin Adams, Jr.

"Little Orphan Annie," starring Shirley Bell

"Myrt and Marge," starring Myrtle Vail and Donna Damerel Fick

"Metropolitan Opera Broadcast" hosted by Milton Cross

"The American Album of Familiar Music," with Donald Dame

Buck Rogers fans saved their Cocomalt boxtops this year. When they had enough, they sent away for "interplanetary maps," thereby qualifying them to become "solar scouts."

Speaking from a bathysphere, WILLIAM BEEBE broadcast from 2,200 feet under the ocean.

THOMAS EDISON

DEATHS

Kenneth "Knute" Rockne, Notre Dame head football coach, famed for his inspirational "Win One for the Gipper" speech, died in a plane crash March 31, in Cottonwood Falls, KS. The head of the "Fighting Irish" was 43.

Thomas Edison, "The Wizard of Menlo Park" and genius behind the phonograph, incandescent lamp, and a thousand other inventions, died October 18 in West Orange, NJ, at 84.

Tyrone Power, Broadway matinee idol and father of Tyrone Power, Jr., died December 30.

"Legs" Diamond, elegantly dressed bootlegger, killer, and gangster, was shot and killed by other mobsters in Albany, NY, December 18.

Kahlil Gibran, Lebanese-born poet, author of *The Prophet,* one of the best-known works of verse in the world, died at 48 April 10 in New York City.

Anna Pavlova, the most celebrated dancer of her time, died January 23 in the Netherlands. During her lifetime, the Russian dancer wowed audiences on both sides of the Atlantic.

celeb births

MICKEY MANTLE, New York Yankee legend, was born October 20 in Spavinaw, OK.

BARBARA WALTERS, talk show host, the first woman to coanchor the "Today Show," was born September 25 in Boston.

TONI MORRISON, author, awarded the Pulitzer Prize for her novel *Beloved,* was born in Lorain, OH, February 18.

BORIS YELTSIN, the first popularly elected president in Russia's thousand-year history, was born February 1 in Butka, USSR.

ROBERT DUVALL, actor, was born January 5 in San Diego.

WILLIE MAYS, San Francisco Giants star, the "Say Hey Kid," was born May 6 in Fairfield, Alabama.

JAMES DEAN, actor and icon, the original *Rebel without a Cause,* was born February 8 in Marion, Indiana.

celeb wedding

Aimee Semple McPherson, 38, founder of the Four-Square Gospel Church and a powerful American evangelist, married 30-year-old **David Hutton,** her 250-pound Angelus Temple voice instructor.

milestones

the peanut vendor Don Azpiazu

just a gigolo Ted Lewis

by the river st. marie Kate Smith

minnie the moocher Cab Calloway

stardust Isham Jones

dream a little dream of me Wayne King

out of nowhere Bing Crosby

(there ought to be a) moonlight saving time
Guy Lombardo

just one more chance Bing Crosby

i found a million-dollar baby (in a five and ten
cent store) Fred Waring's Pennsylvanians

hit music

The RCA Victor Company made its first attempt at a long-playing record. The attempt to go beyond the standard three- to four-minute limit on 78-rpm records was technically second.

Having served his apprenticeship with Paul Whiteman, crooner **Bing Crosby** stepped out to become the nation's most popular singer.

Hoagy Carmichael composed "Georgia on My Mind," a jazz standard recorded by popular vocalist Mildred Bailey.

BING CROSBY

fiction

1. **the good earth**
   by pearl s. buck

2. **shadows on the rock**
   by willa cather

3. **a white bird flying**
   by bess streeter aldrich

4. **grand hotel**
   by vicki baum

5. **years of grace**
   by margaret ayer barnes

6. **the road back**
   by erich maria remarque

7. **the bridge of desire**
   by warwick deeping

8. **back street**
   by fannie hurst

9. **finch's fortune**
   by mazo de la roche

10. **maid in waiting**
    by john galsworthy

As the contract bridge craze swept the nation, champion Ely Culbertson cashed in with his two books guaranteed to make even mediocre bridge fanatics into champs.

Pearl Buck won the Pulitzer Prize for *The Good Earth*, the moving story of a Chinese peasant and his wife.

American fascination with the Soviet regime was amply demonstrated in *New Russia's Primer*, M. Ilin's detailed look at the USSR.

nonfiction

books

1. **education of a princess**
   by grand duchess marie

2. **the story of san michele**
   by axel munthe

3. **washington merry-go-round**
   anonymous

4. **boners**
   editors of Viking Press

5. **culbertson's summary**
   by ely culbertson

6. **contract bridge blue book**
   by ely culbertson

7. **fatal interview**
   by edna st. vincent millay

8. **the epic of america**
   by james truslow adams

9. **mexico**
   by stuart chase

10. **new russia's primer**
    by m. ilin

WILLIAM FAULKNER PUBLISHED *SANCTUARY*, HIS FIRST COMMERCIALLY SUCCESSFUL NOVEL.

Edna St. Vincent Millay had a bestseller with *Fatal Interview*, making her the first bestselling writer of poetry since Stephen Vincent Benet during World War I.

EDNA ST. VINCENT MILLAY

BILL TILDEN

In tennis, **Bill Tilden** made his debut as a pro before a crowd of 13,600 fans at Madison Square Garden. France took the Davis Cup for the fifth year running. At Forest Hills, Ellsworth Vines walked away with the title.

IN THE ROSE BOWL, ALABAMA TROUNCED WASHINGTON, 24–0.

In horse racing, jockey **Charley Kurtsinger rode Twenty Grand to victory at the Kentucky Derby.**

sports

In auto racing, Malcolm Campbell set a new land speed record of 245.7 mph at Daytona Beach, FL.

In baseball, Pepper Martin batted .500 as he led the St. Louis Cardinals' "gas house gang" to victory over the Athletics in 7 games. The victory was sweet revenge for the Redbirds, who lost in 1930 to the A's.

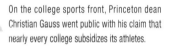

On the college sports front, Princeton dean Christian Gauss went public with his claim that nearly every college subsidizes its athletes.

In boxing, heavyweight **Jack Sharkey** clobbered **Primo Carnera in Brooklyn. Max Schmeling lost the heavyweight title for refusing to fight Sharkey.**

JACK SHARKEY

17

BELA LUGOSI

Monster movies scored big this year. Despite a pronounced lisp, Boris Karloff turned in a chilling performance as the monster in *Frankenstein*. Bela Lugosi played the title role in Tod Browning's **Dracula,** after Lon Chaney died suddenly before shooting began. Lugosi actually hailed from Hungary, a mere bat's flight from Transylvania.

movies

MOVIE THEATERS BEGAN RUNNING DOUBLE FEATURES THIS YEAR, PROVIDING A PLACE FOR THE UNEMPLOYED TO GO DURING THE DAY.

James Cagney showed up as a remorseless, rum-running gangster in his fifth film, *The Public Enemy*.

Laurel and Hardy earned enormous popularity this year. Audiences couldn't get enough of their monumental ineptitude.

OLIVER HARDY AND STAN LAUREL

THE FIFTY MILLIONTH U.S. MOTOR VEHICLE WAS PRODUCED THIS YEAR.

This year automakers faced a dilemma: whether to risk vast sums on completely new models or to reduce drastically the price of existing models. Most automakers stocked the larger, more powerful and luxurious cars that the public had wanted until the Great Depression set in. Dealers offered these big cars at big savings.

A Pierce-Arrow could be had for $810.
An Auburn sold for $945.
You could buy an upscale Buick for $1,025.
And, for the truly profligate, a Cadillac could
be had for $2,695.

cars

A GMC truck and refrigerated trailer delivered 21 tons of California fruit to New York in 117 hours running time. This freezer run demonstrated the efficiency of the "motor truck" as a practical way of transporting perishables.

The 1931 Marmon 16 was a monument to the precision engineering interests of Howard Marmon. The V-16 stood out as a supercar offering the best power-to-weight ratio of any 1931 automobile. Its 490-cubic-inch engine cranked out 200 horsepower. This jumbo engine powered the 6,000-pound custom-bodied classic to 100 miles an hour. A grand total of 390 Marmon V-16s were made, at a selling price of $5,000.

A RETRACTABLE HARDTOP CONVERTIBLE WAS
PATENTED BY B. B. ELLERBECK OF SALT LAKE CITY.

Women were seen with suede gloves—
designed to match their shoes and purse.
Fur—preferably gray or red fox—was
worn over a single shoulder.

**Short, natural hair
parted on the side
was popular with men.
Greasy pomade made
its exit, with most men
favoring water.**

No fashionable woman was without a white satin pajama suit.

fashion

1931 WAS THE YEAR OF THE ACCESSORY.

Accessories for gentlemen included signet ring, cuff links,
cigarette cases, wallets and not one, but two handkerchiefs:
one kept stuffed up the sleeves and one for "show," tucked
in the breast pocket.

Black silk shoes with an ankle strap,
and white suede with a T strap were
both must-wears this season.

**The popular hats this year
sported small brims. Most
were deep and closefitting.
Stylish women pulled them
low over one eye.**

22

6332   6344

IS INTERPRETED IN WAYS UNMISTAKABLY MODERN

No. 6332. Shirrings in front give a Victorian suggestion to a simple frock which is made with a draped collar, a fitted bodice, sleeves that widen at the wrist, and a circular skirt. For back views and yardage see page 95. No. 6344. A flattering type of new dinner dress with a puff at the elbow appears in a simple frock. A flaring peplum adorns a flaring skirt lends grace to a very becoming silhouette.

Patterns may be bought from all McCall dealers, or by mail, postage prepaid, from The McCall Company, McCall Street, Dayton, Ohio, at prices and sizes listed on page 95.

Hair-wise, the most popular styles featured long hair worn
loosely waved with a part on the side. Some women accentuated the look
with a combed roll in back.

23

final
factoid

Alka-Seltzer
went on the market.
It was developed by the editor of an Elkhart, IN, newspaper who gave a dose of aspirin and baking soda to employees coming down with colds.

...thing Quite Like

Alka-Seltzer
BRAND
EFFERVESCENT ANALGESIC ALKALIZING TABLETS

It makes a clear, sparkling alkalizing solution containing an analgesic (acetyl salicylate). You drink it and it gives prompt, pleasant relief for Headaches, ...h, Distress after Meals, Colds and other minor Aches and Pains. 50c PKGS. ALL DRUG STORES—*Slightly higher in Canada*

LISTEN TO The National Barn Dance On The Radio Every Saturday Night N.B.C. Network.

archive photos: inside front cover, pages 1, 6, inside back cover

associated press: pages 2, 3, 5, 10, 15, 16, 17

photofest: pages 8, 9, 13, 18, 19

gaslight: pages 20, 23

bayer corporation: pages 24, 25

photo research:
alice albert

coordination:
rustyn birch

design:
carol bokuniewicz design
paul ritter